Faith Begins @ Home
PRAYER

From personal quiet time to mealtime and even "text message prayers," this resource provides busy moms and dads with solid advice on how to ensure that prayer is put in its proper place: at the very center of the home.

Jim Daly
President and CEO, Focus on the Family

As a senior pastor, Mark Holmen demonstrated how a local church can inspire and equip families to instill strong faith in the next generation. As a partner in the Strong Families Innovation Alliance, he has also been a mentor to other leaders trying to turn the tide of declining generational faith transference.

Kurt Bruner
Executive Director, Strong Families Innovation Alliance

Mark Holmen is energizing families to grow their faith in the home. Mark and his message is one of the freshest and most practical voices among Christian leaders. This resource is helping us follow the mandate of God to pass on our faith from generation to generation.

Jim Burns, Ph.D.
President, HomeWord
Senior Director of the Center for Youth and Family at Azusa Pacific University

Mark leads us not only to the power of prayer in the life of a believer but to the heart of what Faith@Home really is: Modeling these core disciplines to the next generation. With prayer such a personal practice, this resource will help moms and dads learn ways to encourage and model prayer before a generation desperately in need of a deeper connection with their living Savior.

Pastor Greg McCombs
Director of the Canadian Marriage & Family Network
Faith@Home Coach

Mark Holmen clearly knows what spiritual development in the family should look like and how to communicate that message in an engaging way. Parents who digest the four Faith Begins @ Home booklets will have their vision lifted, their hearts warmed, and their minds focused on the practical things they can do to see their children embrace Christ for a lifetime.

Richard Ross, Ph.D.
Professor of Student Ministry at Southwestern Seminary
Fort Worth, Texas

Mark Holmen is providing much-needed leadership in the Faith@Home movement that is sweeping our nation. These resources are excellent tools in that they both challenge and equip parents as they seek to disciple their own children.

Steve Stroope
Lead Pastor, Lake Pointe Church
Rockwall, Texas

Mark Holmen

Author, *Faith Begins at Home* and Founder of Faith @ Home Ministries

Faith Begins @Home PRAYER

Regal

From Gospel Light
Ventura, California, U.S.A.

Published by Regal
From Gospel Light
Ventura, California, U.S.A.
www.regalbooks.com
Printed in the U.S.A.

Library of Congress Cataloging-in-Publication Data
Holmen, Mark.
Faith begins @ home prayer / Mark Holmen.
p. cm.
ISBN 978-0-8307-5211-9 (trade paper)
1. Prayer—Christianity. 2. Families—Religious life. I. Title.
II. Title: Faith begins at home prayer.
BV210.3.H65 2010
248.3'2—dc22
2009044685)

2 3 4 5 6 7 8 9 10 / 16 15 14 13 12 11

Rights for publishing this book outside the U.S.A. or in non-English languages are administered by Gospel Light Worldwide, an international not-for-profit ministry. For additional information, please visit www.glww.org, email info@glww.org, or write to Gospel Light Worldwide, 1957 Eastman Avenue, Ventura, CA 93003, U.S.A.

I dedicate this resource to the two people I know who pray best: My wife, Maria, and my daughter, Malyn. Thank you for praying for me and with me through the years. I love you both and can't wait to see how our prayer life continues to grow in the years ahead.

Contents

Introduction

Welcome to the @ Home series of resources!

This series of booklets has been created for one simple reason: to help you bring true, life-enhancing Christian faith into the fabric of your everyday life at home.

If you are at all like the thousands of parents I have worked with over the past 15-plus years, you have a strong and even desperate desire to establish a more stable and healthy household than the one in which you grew up. I believe that parents today want to be good—if not great—parents, and they want their children to grow up in a supportive and nurturing home environment. Parents today are open to bringing more of God into their lifestyle at home because they know that God can help them; but they simply don't know how to get more of God in their home because it wasn't a part of the home environment they grew up in. Does that description sound familiar to you?

I do not believe the problem that many families face today is due to bad or ungodly parenting. Parents are unprepared to raise their children spiritually because Satan has been at work for the last 40 to 50 years to take Christ and Christ-like living out of the home. Let me be very clear: God wants what's best for you and your family. He wants you and your family to "enjoy long life" (Deuteronomy 6:2), and He has made provision for it. Yet His adversary, the devil "prowls around like a roaring lion looking for someone to devour" (1 Peter 5:8). And one of the areas he prowls is your home.

Satan does not want you living out your faith at home. He does not want you praying, reading the Bible or engaging in faith talk in your home, because he does not want what is best for you and your family. His plan is to get you to believe that faith is something you outsource to the "experts" or express only when you are at church. This is a lie, and it comes from "the father of lies" (John 8:44).

Unfortunately, this thinking creates a hypocritical reality where Christianity is something that we do at church but not at home. Many young adults are walking away from the faith in alarming numbers because they grew up in this hypocritical environment. They are saying, "If that is what Christianity is, then I don't want anything to do with it."

A *New York Times* article reported that in spite of packed megachurches, "evangelical Christian leaders are warning one another that their teenagers are abandoning the faith in droves. At an unusual series of leadership meetings in 44 cities . . . more than 6,000 pastors are hearing dire forecasts from some of the biggest names in the conservative evangelical movement. Their alarm has been stoked by a . . . claim that if current trends continue, only 4 percent of teenagers will be 'Bible-believing Christians' as adults. That would be a sharp decline compared with 35 percent of the current generation of baby boomers, and before that, 65 percent of the World War II generation."[1]

The good news is that we serve a God of second chances. The God of the universe is again offering us the same basic faith skills that will help us, our children and our children's children enjoy long (eternal) life (see Deuteronomy 6:2).

Do you want to enjoy long, eternal life?

Do you want this for your children and your children's children?

Start looking at how you can bring faith back into the very center of your home!

This @ Home booklet will help you and your family establish one specific faith skill with multiple practical applications you can incorporate into your "at home" lifestyle. The content of this booklet assumes that you have no idea how to do this faith skill at home, because research indicates that even Christian households are not actively engaged in these basic faith practices. You will read some compelling and inspirational stories of people who have had their lives transformed as a result of making this faith skill a part of their 24/7 lifestyle. And finally, you will find many practical ideas that apply to all ages and will allow you to establish and maintain this faith skill in your home throughout the years.

May the Lord bless you as you establish your home as the primary place where faith is nurtured.

Note

1. Laurie Goodstein, "Evangelicals Fear the Loss of Their Teen-agers," *New York Times*, October 10, 2006. http://www.nytimes.com/2006/10/06/us/06evangelical.html.

1

The Bible and Prayer

Prayer is at the very core of a personal relationship with Jesus Christ. Why? Prayer is conversation with God. How can you maintain a relationship with someone you never talk to? Yet many people misunderstand prayer. When they think of prayer, they think of a pastor praying a lengthy, well-worded, well-organized prayer that seems to be more of a mini-sermon than a simple dialogue with another Person.

Some people are intimidated by prayer and are afraid to pray out loud or with others. This uncomfortable feeling directly affects whether they pray at home with their family. It affects how they pray and how often they pray at home.

You might think that people who love God and have a definite belief in the saving, sustaining power of Jesus Christ would not have difficulty talking to Him. Yet George Barna, a leading marketing researcher on the intersection of faith and culture in America "discovered that in a typical week, fewer than 10 percent of parents who regularly attend church with their kids read the Bible together, pray together (other than at meal times) or participate in an act of service as a family unit."[1]

Is that your experience? If you're not praying with your family on a regular basis, you are in the majority! While that's not necessarily the best way to live, at least you can take some comfort in the fact that you are not alone. And consider the positive fact that you are reading this resource with a desire to make changes, wherever you are in your faith journey. So, any step you take in that direction will positively impact your life and the lives of every member of your family.

We have established that talking to God is vital to having a relationship with Him. We saw in the Introduction that it is more a matter of knowing what to do than not having any desire to make prayer a natural part of your family life. There is a basis to all of this in God's Word. He hasn't left you to figure these things out all on your own. So let's begin by taking a stroll through Scripture to see what it says about prayer so we can have a clear understanding from God's perspective. The Bible describes for us what prayer is, how we should pray and what people often do in prayer.

What Is Prayer?

Calling Upon the Name of the Lord

Who do you turn to in times of need? Prayer is an opportunity to talk to God about your situation and turn it over to Him. God tells you to call on Him. He desires relationship with you. Here are some examples of how God wants us to live in relation to Him:

- "From there he [Abram] went on toward the hills east of Bethel and pitched his tent, with Bethel on the west and Ai on the east. There he built an altar to the LORD and called on the name of the LORD" (Genesis 12:8).

- "God is our refuge and strength, an ever-present help in trouble" (Psalm 46:1).

- "Call upon me in the day of trouble; I will deliver you, and you will honor me" (Psalm 50:15).

- "Then I called on the name of the LORD: 'O LORD, save me!' " (Psalm 116:4).

- "I lift up my eyes to the hills—where does my help come from? My help comes from the LORD, the Maker of heaven and earth" (Psalm 121:1-2).

Pouring Out Your Heart

Is there anything you've been trying to handle on your own but you need to tell God about it? Remember, God knows what's on your heart. You don't need to hold it in. Pour it out. Give it to Him. Share your life with Him. The Bible records the words of some people who poured out their hearts to God.

- "To you, O LORD, I lift up my soul" (Psalm 25:1).

- "Trust in him at all times, O people; pour out your hearts to him, for God is our refuge" (Psalm 62:8).

- "Arise, cry out in the night, as the watches of the night begin; pour out your heart like water in the presence of the Lord" (Lamentations 2:19).

- "Let us lift up our hearts and our hands to God in heaven" (Lamentations 3:41).

Crying Out to God

Have you ever faced situations where you have cried out, "Why, God? What are You doing, God? Where are you, God? God, what do You want me to do?" The Bible teaches that you have permission to cry out to God, expressing absolutely any emotion you are feeling. It's okay. God is big enough to handle it, so don't hold back.

- "In my distress I called to the LORD; I called out to my God. From his temple he heard my voice; my cry came to his ears" (2 Samuel 22:7).

- "Give attention to your servant's prayer and his plea for mercy, O LORD my God. Hear the cry and the prayer that your servant is praying in your presence" (2 Chronicles 6:19).

- "King Hezekiah and the prophet Isaiah son of Amoz cried out in prayer to heaven about this" (2 Chronicles 32:20).

- "In my distress I called to the LORD; I cried to my God for help. From his temple he heard my voice; my cry came before him, into his ears" (Psalm 18:6).

- "Hear my voice when I call, O LORD; be merciful to me and answer me" (Psalm 27:7).

- "This poor man called, and the LORD heard him; he saved him out of all his troubles" (Psalm 34:6).

Drawing Near to God and Seeking Him

It is easy in this fast-paced world to get far from God. But remember that it's never God who pulls away from you, although you may pull away from Him. Prayer draws you back in close to God. If you feel far from God, it is time to start praying.

- "My heart says of you, 'Seek his face!' Your face, LORD, I will seek" (Psalm 27:8).

- "But as for me, it is good to be near God. I have made the Sovereign LORD my refuge" (Psalm 73:28).

- "Let us draw near to God with a sincere heart in full assurance of faith, having our hearts sprinkled to cleanse us from a guilty conscience" (Hebrews 10:22).

Making Supplication

God invites you to ask Him for things. You can ask God to provide a job for your spouse or healing for a relative or a friend who is battling cancer. Why wouldn't you ask God to help? Who better to ask than God?

- "Give attention to your servant's prayer and his plea for mercy, O LORD my God. Hear the cry and the prayer that your servant is praying in your presence this day" (1 Kings 8:28).

- "Then hear from heaven their prayer and their plea, and uphold their cause" (2 Chronicles 6:35).

- "Perhaps they will bring their petition before the LORD, and each will turn from his wicked ways, for the anger and wrath pronounced against this people by the LORD are great" (Jeremiah 36:7).

- "Do not be anxious about anything, but in everything, by prayer and petition, with thanksgiving, present your requests to God" (Philippians 4:6).

How Should We Pray?

A second area the Bible describes is how prayer should be offered to Him. Prayer is heart communication with God. The Bible describes how we should pray.

Pray in Full Assurance of Faith and Confidence in God

True faith is trusting God when you don't have all the answers. God hears your prayers. He responds according to His plan and purpose, which is perfect and greater than you can fully understand.

- "My enemies will turn back when I call for help. By this I will know that God is for me" (Psalm 56:9).

- "In the day of my trouble I will call to you, for you will answer me" (Psalm 86:7).

- "If you believe, you will receive whatever you ask for in prayer" (Matthew 21:22).

- "Let us draw near to God with a sincere heart in full assurance of faith" (Hebrews 10:22).

- "When he asks, he must believe and not doubt, because he who doubts is like a wave of the sea, blown and tossed by the wind" (James 1:6).

- "This is the confidence we have in approaching God: that if we ask anything according to his will, he hears us" (1 John 5:14).

Pray with Submission to God

When asking, remember that you are praying for God's will to be done, not yours. Determine to remain faithful even when His will is different from yours. God has all eternity to explain things, and He will.

- "Jesus went out as usual to the Mount of Olives, and his disciples followed him. He withdrew about a stone's throw beyond them, knelt down and prayed, 'Father, if you are willing, take this cup from me; yet not my will, but yours be done'" (Luke 22:39,41-42).

- "Submit yourselves, then, to God. Resist the devil, and he will flee from you. Come near to God and he will come near to you" (James 4:7-8).

Pray Continually and Earnestly

Just keep praying . . . just keep praying . . . just keep praying.

- "Night and day we pray most earnestly that we may see you again and supply what is lacking in your faith" (1 Thessalonians 3:10).

- "Pray continually" (1 Thessalonians 5:17).

- "The widow who is really in need and left all alone puts her hope in God and continues night and day to pray and to ask God for help" (1 Timothy 5:5).

- "Elijah was a man just like us. He prayed earnestly that it would not rain, and it did not rain on the land for three and a half years" (James 5:17).

Pray with Humility

God is God, and you are not. Remember who you are and who God is. He is your Father; you are His child. He knows how you were formed and the number of days that make up your lifetime.

- "If my people, who are called by my name, will humble themselves and pray and seek my face and turn from their wicked ways, then will I hear from heaven and will forgive their sin and will heal their land" (2 Chronicles 7:14).

- "In his distress he sought the favor of the LORD his God and humbled himself greatly before the God of his fathers" (2 Chronicles 33:12).

Pray with a Desire to be Heard

When you speak, you have God's attention. He wants to hear what you have to say.

- "Let your ear be attentive and your eyes open to hear the prayer your servant is praying before you day and night for your servants, the people of Israel. I confess the sins we Israelites, including myself and my father's house, have committed against you" (Nehemiah 1:6).

- "Hear, O LORD, my righteous plea; listen to my cry. Give ear to my prayer—it does not rise from deceitful lips" (Psalm 17:1)

- "Listen to my prayer, O God, do not ignore my plea; hear me and answer me. My thoughts trouble me and I am distraught" (Psalm 55:1-2).

- "Hear my cry, O God; listen to my prayer" (Psalm 61:1).

Pray with Boldness and a Desire to Be Answered

Pray expecting something to happen.

- "Hear my voice when I call, O LORD; be merciful to me and answer me" (Psalm 27:7).

- "Do not hide your face from me when I am in distress. Turn your ear to me; when I call, answer me quickly" (Psalm 102:2).

- "Save us and help us with your right hand, that those you love may be delivered" (Psalm 108:6).

- "Let us then approach the throne of grace with confidence, so that we may receive mercy and find grace to help us in our time of need" (Hebrews 4:16).

Then we have the ultimate biblical text example of how to pray, which is found in Luke 11, where Jesus taught His disciples—and us—how to pray:

One day Jesus was praying in a certain place. When he finished, one of his disciples said to him, "Lord, teach us to pray, just as John taught his disciples." He said to them, "When you pray, say: 'Father, hallowed be your name, your kingdom come. Give us each day our daily bread. Forgive us our sins, for we also forgive everyone who sins against us. And lead us not into temptation.'" Then he said to them, "Suppose one of you has a friend, and he goes to him at midnight and says, 'Friend, lend me three loaves of bread, because a friend of mine on a journey has come to me, and I have nothing to set before him.' Then the one inside answers, 'Don't bother me. The door is already locked, and my children are with me in bed. I can't get up and give you anything.' I tell you, though he will not get up and give him the bread because he is his friend, yet because of the man's boldness he will get up and give him as much as he needs. So I say to you: Ask and it will be given to you; seek and you will find; knock and the door will be opened to you. For everyone who asks receives; he who seeks finds; and to him who knocks, the door will be opened. Which of you fathers, if your son asks for a fish, will give him a snake instead? Or if he asks for an egg, will give him a scorpion? If you then, though you are evil, know how to give good gifts to your children,

how much more will your Father in heaven
give the Holy Spirit to those who ask him!"
(Luke 11:1-13).

Jesus did two things in this teaching: First, He
gave us a very practical, repeatable prayer that pretty
much covers everything that needs to be covered
and keeps us focused on the things that we should
be praying for. Yet, immediately after this, Jesus
went on to say that you do not have to confine yourself to this prayer. Essentially, Jesus said, pray this
prayer and also pray for whatever is on your heart.
So when it comes to describing how to pray, the
door is wide open.

Prayer—and Beyond

The Bible also describes other actions that often ac-
company prayer.

Confession and Repentance

Often, we don't approach God in prayer because we
feel out of step, even if we don't quite know what's
wrong. But chances are good that the problem has
to do with a wrong attitude or outright sinful action. God already knows what the issue is, but He's
set up relationship with Him in such a way that only
if we confess it to Him and turn away from (repent
of) the wrong attitude or action can we be restored
to closeness with Him once again.

- "When your people Israel have been defeated by an enemy because they have sinned against you, and when they turn back to you and confess your name, praying and making supplication to you in this temple, then hear from heaven and forgive the sin of your people Israel and bring them back to the land you gave to their fathers" (1 Kings 8:33-34).

- "When I heard these things, I sat down and wept. For some days I mourned and fasted and prayed before the God of heaven. Then I said: 'O LORD, God of heaven, the great and awesome God, who keeps his covenant of love with those who love him and obey his commands, let your ear be attentive and your eyes open to hear the prayer your servant is praying before you day and night for your servants, the people of Israel. I confess the sins we Israelites, including myself and my father's house, have committed against you. We have acted very wickedly toward you. We have not obeyed the commands, decrees and laws you gave your servant Moses'" (Nehemiah 1:4-7).

- "Perhaps they will bring their petition before the LORD, and each will turn from his wicked ways, for the anger and wrath pronounced against this people by the LORD are great" (Jeremiah 36:7).

- "I prayed to the LORD my God and confessed: 'O Lord, the great and awesome God, who keeps his covenant of love with all who love him and obey his commands, we have sinned and done wrong. We have been wicked and have rebelled; we have turned away from your commands and laws. We have not listened to your servants the prophets, who spoke in your name to our kings, our princes and our fathers, and to all the people of the land. Lord, you are righteous, but this day we are covered with shame—the men of Judah and people of Jerusalem and all Israel, both near and far, in all the countries where you have scattered us because of our unfaithfulness to you. O LORD, we and our kings, our princes and our fathers are covered with shame because we have sinned against you. The Lord our God is merciful and forgiving, even though we have rebelled against him; we have not obeyed the LORD our God or kept the laws he gave us through his servants the prophets. All Israel has transgressed your law and turned away, refusing to obey you' " (Daniel 9:4-11).

Weeping

Much of what you face in life is emotional, so you don't need to keep your emotions out of your prayer life. God knows you intimately (see Psalm 139 and Acts 15:8), and "He knows the secrets of the heart" (Psalm 44:21).

- "They will come with weeping; they will pray as I bring them back. I will lead them beside streams of water on a level path where they will not stumble" (Jeremiah 31:9).

- "He struggled with the angel and overcame him; he wept and begged for his favor" (Hosea 12:4).

Watchfulness

When Jesus rose into heaven, the angels told His followers, "This same Jesus, who has been taken from you into heaven, will come back in the same way you have seen him go into heaven" (Acts 1:11). Pray as if Jesus is coming back at any time.

- "Be always on the watch, and pray that you may be able to escape all that is about to happen, and that you may be able to stand before the Son of Man" (Luke 21:36).

- "The end of all things is near. Therefore be clear minded and self-controlled so that you can pray" (1 Peter 4:7).

Praise and Thanksgiving

Think of all the things you can give God thanks and praise for. He has so generously provided for you that this could easily consume all of your prayer time!

- "I cried out to him with my mouth; his praise was on my tongue" (Psalm 66:17).

- "Do not be anxious about anything, but in everything, by prayer and petition, with thanksgiving, present your requests to God" (Philippians 4:6).

- "Devote yourselves to prayer, being watchful and thankful" (Colossians 4:2).

I have not provided an exhaustive list of what the Bible has to say on prayer, but only a quick overview of what prayer is and how to pray. Read the Bible, paying attention to how it describes prayer. Read books about prayer and the power of prayer. (Visit www.faithbeginsathome.com for some great prayer resources you can use at home.) As you continue to explore this topic, your eyes and heart will be opened, increasing your prayer life even further.

Prayer is a personal expression of desires and longings from your heart to God's. A well-known hymn describes this kind of prayer as sharing heart-to-heart with Jesus as a Friend.

What a Friend We Have in Jesus

What a Friend we have in Jesus,
all our sins and griefs to bear!
What a privilege to carry
everything to God in prayer!
O what peace we often forfeit,
O what needless pain we bear,
All because we do not carry
everything to God in prayer.

Have we trials and temptations?
Is there trouble anywhere?
We should never be discouraged;
take it to the Lord in prayer.
Can we find a friend so faithful
who will all our sorrows share?
Jesus knows our every weakness;
take it to the Lord in prayer.

Are we weak and heavy laden,
cumbered with a load of care?
Precious Savior, still our refuge,
take it to the Lord in prayer.
Do your friends despise, forsake you?
Take it to the Lord in prayer!
In His arms He'll take and shield you;
you will find a solace there.

Blessed Savior, Thou hast promised
Thou wilt all our burdens bear
May we ever, Lord, be bringing all to

Thee in earnest prayer.
Soon in glory bright unclouded there
will be no need for prayer
Rapture, praise and endless worship
will be our sweet portion there.

Words: Joseph Scriven (1857)

Note

1. George Barna, *Transforming Children into Spiritual Champions* (Ventura, CA: Regal Books, 2003).

2

Why Pray?

Before you take the next step of prayer with your family, take a moment to assess your family's prayer life. Have each person in your family rate each of the following three statements on a scale from 0 to 5 (0 is the lowest degree, or interest; 5 is the highest degree, or interest).

- Our family supports each other in prayer.
- I am satisfied with how and when our family prays together.
- I am open to learning new ways to pray with my children.

One of the things I quickly discovered as a youth and family ministry pastor was not to assume anything regarding prayer life in the home. Some families that I would not have expected to have a great prayer life at home did pray together, while others that I assumed were strong pray-ers never engaged in prayer at home. Even in the families that did pray together, I found there was great diversity in how prayer was handled in each home.

Consider the following stories of two different families. Can you see your family in either one of them?

The phone rang in my office at the church. It was Alan, a member of the congregation. We greeted each other at church, but he rarely called, so I presumed something was wrong.

He searched for the right words. "I'm having troubles with my 15-year-old, Andrea."

"What do you mean by troubles?" I asked.

"We're not communicating well, and it seems like we're on opposite ends of every situation."

Realizing that he needed more than a quick answer, I went to visit him. Alan, his wife and two children lived in a beautiful home. By the world's standards they had everything together. Alan was involved in committees at the church, and his wife helped out with Sunday School. His daughter, Andrea, was actively involved in the youth program, and she helped teach Sunday School.

I spent the first 30 minutes in his home listening to story after story of how disrespectful Andrea had become.

"She doesn't listen to me anymore," he exclaimed. "And when I establish a rule or guideline, she pushes it to the limit and further, which forces me to do something about it. I'm also concerned about the friends she's hanging out with, and I'm wondering if I need to limit how much time she spends with them."

As he continued sharing his concerns, I remember thinking, *What am I going to say? I don't have a teenager and have never had to face this myself.*

Finally, Alan asked, "What am I supposed to do?"

Not wanting to let on that I was feeling ill-equipped to handle the situation, I turned to God for help. I sat back in the chair and then asked, "Have you prayed with your daughter about this?"

This didn't seem like a ludicrous question to me, because I had seen Alan lead prayer numerous times at committee meetings, and his daughter led prayer in Sunday School every Sunday. Yet, when I asked the question, the look in his eyes told me all I needed to know. Over the first 15 years of his daughter's life, Alan was actively involved in taking her to daycare, soccer practice, piano lessons and even church, but he had not once prayed with his daughter. The idea of praying with his daughter for the first time seemed utterly beyond the scope of reason to him.

The situation in Alan's family is reality in many families today. Most families are two or three generations removed from the last generation that remembers what it was like to have prayer, Bible reading and devotions as an integral part of life at home. The reason people are not praying at home is not because they don't want to. The reason is because they don't know how to do it. As a result of seeing this need and desire in so many parents to spiritually nurture their children at home, our church realized we had to become more intentional in equipping people to live out their faith at home. As a part of that emphasis, we began offering Take It Home training events for parents and their young children on the topic of prayer.[1]

Here's another home situation that might be like yours. I'll never forget when Dan and Wendy came to the Take It Home event on prayer. I had never seen Dan before, but I could see he was not very excited to be there. Dan's only experience with Christianity was an occasional visit to a Sunday or Saturday evening mass with his family. He had given up going to church altogether for the past eight years. Wendy, after the birth of their first child, realized she needed God and wanted to raise her children in church. She became very involved at our church.

At the time of the prayer event, Dan and Wendy had a five-year-old son and three-year-old daughter. Those kids were their pride and joy. Dan and Wendy made a good living, had a nice house and provided a fairly stable home environment for their children. Yet the more involved Wendy became in her faith the more she yearned to have Dan be a part of their spiritual life. Every time she suggested Dan attend church he would politely, but definitely, reject the offer.

As a part of our Sunday School program, parents are asked to come one Sunday a year with their children for a Take It Home event to learn a faith skill they can incorporate into their home life. As that Sunday approached, Wendy asked Dan if he would attend the Take It Home event on prayer with her and their son, Nate. When Dan asked what it was, Wendy told him she wasn't sure but knew it was to help them as parents. "They are asking all of the parents of five-year-olds to come with their kids."

"Sounds like a trick just to get us to church," Dan replied. "You go. Church is a thing for you and the kids anyway."

Wendy made one more attempt. "Our anniversary is coming up, and I know you haven't gotten me anything yet. Do you know the gift I would like the most this year?"

"What's that?" Dan replied.

"I would like you to go to this Take It Home event with me. That's all I want this year—one hour of your time to go with me and Nate to this event at church."

Dan paused. "Okay, if it's that important to you, I'll go."

Wendy was thrilled.

During the event, I watched Dan and Wendy join their son Nate as they learned how to do mealtime prayers, bedtime prayers and anytime prayers together. It was fun to watch them sing the mealtime prayer, which is sung to the "Superman" tune. It ended up being Nate's favorite. At the end of the event, Dan and Wendy received a handout with 14 ways to pray with their kids at home. They left with smiles on their faces. Little did I know then what God would do in their lives as a result of this one event.

Fast-forward four years and imagine the same Take It Home event for parents and five-year-olds.

Dan and Wendy are also there. Why? So that Dan could share their testimony.

Dan, with his wife and son at his side, gets up and says, "My name is Dan, and I would like to tell you my story. I attended this event on prayer four years ago with my wife and son. To be perfectly honest, I didn't want to be here. In fact, the reason I came was because my wife said it was the only thing she wanted as an anniversary present. I figured coming to this was a lot less expensive than a night out on the town!

"Growing up, I didn't have much experience praying. I felt uneasy about praying with my kids. But during this event, I learned so many fun and easy ways to pray, and I found myself getting into it. It's been four years, and a favorite part of my day is when I pray with my nine-year-old in his bedroom before he goes to bed. He won't even go to bed until we pray, and I'm glad. Give prayer a chance and you may discover it's one of the best things that could ever happen in your family."

Dan and Wendy are now members of our church. They have taken to heart and put into practice all the faith skills offered through the Take It Home events. As a family, they worship, pray and have family devotions together. They have just begun doing a monthly service project together as a family. Dan recently said to me, "I didn't know Christianity could be so much fun and helpful all at the same time."

Are you still asking the question, Why pray? You can choose not to pray in your home and then when trouble hits, like it did for Alan and his daughter, you won't have it as a resource to draw upon to help you through. Or you can make prayer a part of your family life today, which will help you weather the storms by keeping lines of communication open between your family members and God. Wherever you are in your prayer experience in your home, you can benefit from learning to keep prayer fresh and alive. God wants you and your family to enjoy long, everlasting life. Let's start praying.

Note
1. Visit www.gospellight.com for the Take It Home resource that equips churches to offer Take It Home events for parents and children.

3

Let's Pray

Your family prayer time is a perfect opportunity to nurture the spiritual development of your children. As you model prayer, you are growing as a believer, and your children are learning about having conversation with God and shaping their understanding about God and prayer. You are making disciples in your own home. The main thing is to be sensitive to the personality differences in family members and their preferences, and don't let those differences keep you from praying together every day. A few prayer principles will help you better understand how to make family prayer work well for your family.

People Are at Different Places in Their Prayer Life

Some in your family may never have prayed aloud. Don't put pressure on them to pray in a certain way. Avoid rewarding or judging those with more or less experience in the way they pray out loud. It is important to give permission for people to pray in their own way. For example, my wife, Maria, never saw her dad pray, other than at church when she was growing up. But after we had been married a few years, she had a conversation with her dad about prayer, and he revealed something she never knew. He said, "I never listened to radio once in my 30 years of driving to and from work. That 25-minute drive was my time to pray. On the way to work I would pray for you, your brother, your mom and anything else we had going on as a family. And on the way back from work, I would express thanksgiving for everything God had given us. So while you've never seen me pray, I have been praying for you every day."

Was that wrong for him to pray in that manner? Absolutely not. I wish more people would take prayer that seriously. Give each other room to pray in the manner that best suits you.

Having said that, when you pray out loud often with your young children, you give them a model to replicate. Don't be surprised if you hear them pray the exact phrases or prayers they have heard you pray, or if their prayers are always the same every time. As they grow and develop, their vocabulary and expressions of prayer will expand as well. Praying with and in front of your older children lets them know you care deeply for them and enhances the quality of their spiritual lives.

Your child's personality will come out through prayer styles. If your child is very verbal, talking all the time, his or her prayers will probably reflect that same talkative nature. Some children are more reserved and you feel as if you have to pump them for information every time you want them to talk. They may be quieter as they pray until they become comfortable and feel safe praying with the family.

Prayer Is an Important Component in All Households

Don't neglect prayer just because it isn't easy to please everyone. While you need to give family members space and permission to pray in their own way, you still need to make a commitment to pray together. How great it would have been for my wife to have had the opportunity to pray with her dad when he drove to and from work! This is what I would call a "pray in their way" approach.

Be willing to engage in each other's most comfortable form of prayer and you may find that you like their form of prayer better than you thought you would. Ask other family members to pray in ways that may not be comfortable to them as they consider other family members' preferences.

Encourage prayer often in your home. Engage family members of all ages to connect with God wherever they are and talk with Him about whatever is going on in their lives. Lead out in prayer so your children will eventually learn how to talk to God themselves. Look for opportunities to pray anytime you are all together. Pray in the car before heading down the road on vacation. Take a moment to pray for families in the other cars. Pray briefly together every time you hear ambulance or fire truck sirens. The more you pray together, the more natural it will feel.

Prayer Is About Turning to God for the Answers

Prayer is turning to God for the answers rather than thinking you have to know it all yourself. One of the concerns that parents may have in bringing faith into the center of their home is the fear their children will ask a question they don't know how to answer. That's the beauty of prayer. It gives you a chance to turn these questions and concerns over to God. We don't have the answers. It's okay to admit it in prayer.

Recently, one of my best friends was released from his job without any warning after he had served his employer faithfully for over nine years. While the economy was blamed for the release, it was still handled in a manner that did not show the respect he deserved for his loyalty. That evening, my daughter and I prayed for him, and we had to admit in prayer that we did not understand why he had to lose his job. We shared with God our concerns for him and his family. We asked God to give them peace until He would reveal why He had allowed it to happen.

Before we prayed, we felt frustrated, angry and fearful of what would happen. After our prayer time, we had peace because we knew God was in control. While we didn't have the answers, we remembered that God did.

Think in Terms of Personal Development

Move gradually forward in your prayer life, expecting growth in yourself and your family members. Appreciate progress and anticipate change.

I don't pray the same way today I did 10 years ago. I'm sure I won't be praying the same way 10 years from now. Prayer is a way to grow closer to God and to others. As you grow, you change. Unfortunately, everyone changes and grows at a different pace, and you need to realize that your family prayer life will always be a growing and changing thing. Celebrate change and support one another's spiritual growth spurts.

Some of the prayer differences will have to do with the developmental level of your family members. Young children with limited vocabulary and cognitive development will have more limited expressions of prayer. Things that seem trivial to you, like little boo-boos you can't even see on your children's fingers, are huge issues for them. Use your prayer time with them to teach them they are very special to God, and He cares about the things that matter to them. As they develop and mature in all ways, God's care is one message that will remain constant for them no matter what issues concern them the most.

Nothing makes a father prouder than listening to his child grow in prayer. I've watched my friends Kim and Warren enjoy watching their son Tanner pray wonderful prayers. For a while, my daughter, Malyn, was not comfortable praying in front of others at mealtime, and we honored her by not asking her to pray in those environments. Over time she became more comfortable praying out loud, eventually praying in front of others. I love it when we have friends over for dinner and we occasionally ask Malyn to pray, and she prays without any hesitation.

Allow your children to grow at their own rate while encouraging them to pray regularly. Don't rush things. Praying every day will allow them to develop naturally.

Anticipate and Celebrate Diversity

What works with one child may not work with another. One couple we know has four kids, each two years apart in age. Because our church teaches parents how to pray with their four-year-olds, this couple has attended the prayer training four times. The training has not changed much over the years. The focus is to teach families how to do mealtime prayers, bedtime prayers and anytime prayers at home. As this couple planned to attend the training for the fourth time with their youngest daughter, I told the dad that I would understand if he didn't want to come because he already knew what we would be teaching. I'll never forget his response: "Are you kidding? I've done this training three times already, and each time it's turned out different for us. Each of our kids has picked a different mealtime prayer or bedtime prayer that becomes a favorite. I love it. I can't wait to see what my daughter picks! Don't change a thing, and never apologize for having us come multiple times."

Especially if you have children of different ages, be willing to enjoy and try new kinds of prayers to match the differences of everyone in the family. Expect each person to be different and celebrate the way each is unique.

WARNING:
Take and Make Time for Prayer

With busy schedules, it is hard to find a time when everyone can gather for prayer. But don't fall into the trap of thinking or saying, "Let's just do it without him or her. It's easier that way." Just because it may be easier doesn't mean it's best. In fact, often the easier path is usually not the right path. Encourage everyone to participate in family prayer time, even if it is via phone, Internet or silently standing with you.

One way to be sure to pray together every day is to pick a time when everyone is home together. Maybe you will gather together before everyone heads off to school and work. Maybe you will pray every day at breakfast or supper. Maybe your family time is just before the kids go to bed. If you have a standing prayer date, you'll be more likely to incorporate it into your life. You will find lots of other times to pray, too, but a scheduled time for pray is a good basic way to start. It makes praying together a priority for your family.

In addition, there will be times when praying with family members will happen when only two or three are gathered together. Maybe mom or dad spends time with the kids while the other parent is at work. These are ideal times to incorporate a regular prayer time together.

If you discover that it's been a while since you prayed together, don't get discouraged, and don't give up. Just start praying again.

Prayer Develops a Consciousness of God's Presence

Isn't it amazing how easily we can forget that God is with us? We think, How am I going to figure this out? How am I going to get through this? How should I handle this? Where do I turn now? We can get so caught up in our daily routine thinking that it's all about us that we forget there is an all-knowing, all-powerful God we can turn things over to. When was the last time you:

- Truly turned your life situations and issues over to God?

- Sat and did nothing but look and listen for God's presence?
- Waited for God to give an answer before moving forward?
- Opened God's Word and simply read it for pleasure?

One of Satan's trademark tricks is to create noise around us and get us moving fast so we don't have the time or ability to hear the still, small voice of God. Prayer is a time we can shut off the noise of the outside world and reconnect with the God of the universe. Spend some time together with your family in silence, enjoying a beautiful sunset and His presence. It doesn't get much better than that!

Sometimes being aware of God's presence means simply taking time during prayer. Don't feel rushed through your prayer time. Allow for moments of silence and expectant waiting. Prayer is conversation with a Person. If we only talk, it would be like a phone conversation where you call a friend, do all the talking and then quickly hang up and move on. Taking time to listen allows God to speak to our hearts and bring His peace to our situations.

Prayer Brings You Closer as a Family and Increases Communication

When you pray as a family, you will become more aware of what is going on in your family. Some of my best information about what's going on in my daughter's life comes out when we're praying. I find out through her prayers what God is doing in her life and in the lives of her friends. I become more aware of the concerns she has as well as the joys she is experiencing. God is at work in so many ways you cannot see, and prayer can be a way to see how God has been at work. Remember, your children will also gain insight about you and your relationship with God as they hear your prayers. Knowing more about each other should be a positive experience for everyone and something that increases further communication. As you share more of your life and concerns with each other, trust and love will increase, which will make it more natural to pray for one another.

Experience Is the Best Teacher

You don't learn to pray by reading a book. You learn to pray by praying. My wife and I had both grown up in the Midwest playing basketball, so when our school needed coaches for the sixth-grade girls' team, we prayerfully said yes. We were both excited about coaching, and in the weeks leading up to our first practice, we got coaching books, put together a plan for defense and offense and carefully mapped out each practice leading up to our first game. Practices went well even though for most girls this was their first time on a basketball team. They seemed to be picking up on things well. Each week the team got better at drills, and my wife and I became more confident they were going to play great that first game. In fact, I envisioned that we would dominate and win by at least 20 points!

As the tip-off of our first game neared, I gave final instructions and sent them out onto the floor. Thankfully, I had prepared them for the tip-off. Then I watched in utter dismay at all the things they did not know how to do—things that happen only in a game. Things the drills had not taught them. At one point, the ball went out-of-bounds and our team had no idea what to do next. I hadn't taught them an inbounds play. A foul was called. The team needed to line up on the foul line, but none of our girls knew what to do because I hadn't taught them where to stand when someone is shooting a free throw. I learned a lot that first game, and needless to say, we didn't win by 20 points.

In a similar way, you can't learn to pray until you get in the game and start praying. Is it going to feel strange at first? Probably. Will there be times when it's uncomfortable or even embarrassing? In all likelihood. But you will get better, just as our basketball team got better and eventually went on to win the league championship three years later as eighth-graders.

One day, you, too, will look back on your prayer life and say, "Look how far God and I have come." Write down some of your young children's prayers.

In later years, read the prayers back to them and talk about how they have grown in their friendship with God. Encourage your older children to write down some of their prayers and read them again after a few years have passed.

Use a Variety of Ways to Encourage Prayer

Let each person know that God wants praying to be a positive experience. There are many ways to pray, and that makes prayer exciting. God is incredibly creative, and He speaks in many ways. You have multiple ways to speak to Him as well. Think about all the ways you have of expressing your thoughts and feelings to other people. A relationship with God involves various expressions of speaking to a Person.

One of the things I like doing when I am leading a parenting workshop is to simply ask people, "What are some effective ways that you and your family have engaged in prayer?" I am always amazed with some of the ideas I hear. In this book, you will find a variety of ideas for prayer, some of which have been gleaned from others. If you ever find your prayer life getting stalled, simply ask some of your friends how they pray. Ask your children to suggest new and different ways to pray together as a family. Find out what ways are meaningful to them and which bring them closer to God. For a while, I shut the radio off while I drove to and from work and used that as my time to pray. Can you guess where I got that idea?

Before you get started praying together as a family, ask each person to share his or her experience with prayer from earliest recollections to the present. This works best with children who are older and have a prayer history. But don't leave out the young ones. You might be surprised at the level of their communication with God. You may want to be the first to share in order to model what you want others to do. Be honest so your family can see that you, too, are growing in your prayer life.

One of the best things that you can do with your family is to have clear and open communication about prayer so that you can know where everyone is coming from, and so that everyone is comfortable sharing, since prayer is very personal and needs a safe environment. This sharing will establish a common place of understanding for everyone in the family.

You may be surprised to hear how each person has experienced prayer. Through the conversation, ask questions like: When you think of prayer what comes to mind? When do you first remember praying? How has prayer been a part of your life over the years? How is prayer a part of your life now? What has been your best experience with prayer? What difficulties, if any, have you had with prayer?

There you go. Some foundational principles to get you started. Now it's time to get praying!

4

Ways to Pray

As you may already know, there are many ways to pray. Don't get stuck on one form. You can be creative in your prayer times. If your family is like many other families, you will find yourself moving from one style of prayer to another style as your children get older. There is no one right way to pray, so enjoy the freedom and flexibility God has given you in prayer.

Prayers That Are Read

If you go to your local Christian bookstore or search online, you will find all sorts of prayer books that have written prayers in them for all occasions or situations. You can find daily prayer books, topical prayer books, situational prayer books and books that will help you pray through the Scriptures. A hymnal or songbook can be a source of prayers to music.

Look for resources that are geared to the age-level of your children. If you have a broad age-span, from very young children to teenagers, choose a couple of resources so that everyone can participate at their own level of understanding and expression. Praying together may be as simple as reading the prayers from some of these resources and making them your prayers to God. After family members have read their prayers, take a moment to discuss the way these prayers impacted you.

When Mr. McGregor walked up to me following a men's Bible study, I already knew what he is going to say. In his right hand was his personal copy of *The Daily Bread*, a devotional book he keeps inside the front cover of his Bible. "Pastor Mark, you'll never guess what my *Daily Bread* said today. It fits perfectly with the message you just preached." He opened up his *Daily Bread* and read to me the paragraph, short story or prayer he had read that morning. What I love about Mr. McGregor is the fact that he was so excited to read his *Daily Bread* every day. Even though he was in his late seventies, you would think he had just found the secret map to a hidden treasure of gold in his daily spiritual reading.

Do you have a prayer book that is feeding you spiritually every day?

Prayer Requests

In many families, one or more family members are often more comfortable with praying out loud than others. An easy way for these more "seasoned" prayers to get others involved is to begin the prayer time by simply having them ask a series of questions like; "What would you like me to pray for? What do we want to give God praise for? What concerns do we want to take to the Lord today?" Be patient as younger children express their requests. They may have many requests or get sidetracked with extended stories as they explain the situation. When they finish, summarize what they said into a sentence, if possible, so you know that you understood their request, and also to give them a model for summarizing their requests as they mature.

Have a different member of the family write down all the requests that are shared. Keep a record of the requests using a prayer journal like the one found at the end of this book. After everyone has had an opportunity to share, the "seasoned" pray-er prays for all the requests.

The next time you gather for prayer, take the prayer journal and begin by reviewing the previous prayer requests to see how God has been at work in and through your prayer life as a family. Over time you will see how God is answering prayer. Remember, sometimes God answers yes, sometimes no and sometimes wait. Through each answer, your children can learn about God's sovereignty, how He has a bigger plan and that He always works things out for ultimate good to those who love Him and are called to follow Him (see Romans 8:28).

Silent Prayer

Have you ever had to make a major decision or face a difficult reality as a family? How did you handle it?

Did you try to figure it out yourself or did you ask for God's help? Think about what your family is facing or needing to make a decision today, and take it to the Lord in silent prayer. Determine a topic for everyone to pray about and then set aside 2, 3, 5, 10 or even 15 minutes for everyone to pray about it in silence. Give everyone permission to pray in a comfortable place, yet be sure to decide how you will end this time of prayer. Keep your very young children near you during this type of prayer and keep the prayer time brief for them, maybe a minute or two. Explain to them how you pray during this time, and say out loud what you might say in your head so that they can model your silent prayer.

Written Prayers

Some people are better at writing out their prayers than praying out loud. Give everyone about 5 to 10 minutes to write a prayer on a piece of paper. For young children who do not yet read or write, ask them to draw a picture or have them dictate their prayer to you as you write it down. Put each written prayer in an envelope and put the envelopes into a paper bag. Each family member pulls out an envelope and reads the prayer that was written.

One time, my daughter had a school assignment. At the end, she was to conclude her assignment with a written prayer. As I read what she wrote, I was moved to tears at what she had written, because I was able to see into the spiritual heart of my child. Sometimes a written prayer provides a chance for us to go to a deeper spiritual place in our prayer life.

Give your older children their own prayer journal to record their prayers. Encourage them to continue to keep on praying about these issues until they feel they have some answer from God.

Circle Prayer

In the circle prayer, you are providing an opportunity for everyone to pray while no one is required to pray. Sit or stand in a circle, holding hands. Assign someone to be the "prayer starter/ender." This person begins the prayer time by praying for whatever he or she wants to pray for. When that person is done, he or she squeezes the hand of the person on the left, which indicates that it is now that person's time to pray. That person can pray or squeeze the next person's hand. In either case, the squeezing of the hand indicates that you are done with your turn and it is now the next person's turn. Continue going around the circle until you get back to the "prayer starter/ender" who then concludes the prayer by saying, "And everyone agreed and said, AMEN!"

Another version of the circle prayer that encourages everyone to pray out loud is for each person to share a request and then go around the circle and pray for the request he or she made. Or pray for the person on your left and squeeze that person's hand when you're finished.

Text-Message Prayers

When my daughter turned 13, we entered the "text zone." She received a cell phone with unlimited texting. Communication, as we formerly knew it, drastically changed. Conversations were replaced with one-word replies followed by a question because, as you undoubtedly know, every text message has to end with a question to keep the texting alive! One of my first exchanges with my daughter, which happened while I was in the middle of a home improvement project, began innocently enough. She sent me a simple question. I stopped what I was doing, sent her a short reply, and went back to work. Then I received a second message, asking another question, to which I sent back the five words or less answer, which took me 10 minutes to press out. Just when I got back into the project, another text message beep came from my phone, alerting me of yet another text that I had just received. Finally, after the third or fourth interruption, I finally wrote to my daughter, "Just call me!"

Whether I like to admit it or not, texting is a huge (and many times preferred) means of communication today. Now that a few months have passed, and I have gotten faster, I do have fun texting my daughter. And I have discovered that texting is a way to engage in prayer with family members.

As I'm writing this I am on a plane headed to speak at a series of conferences in Norway and the Netherlands. Just before I left, I was in a final text exchange with my daughter, and this was the last message I received before I had to shut off my phone. (These aren't typos, this is exactly how it was sent to me, which, I'm told, is proper text spelling and punctuation.) *"Have fun! may God bless u and keep u. may his face shine upon u and b gracious to you. may he give u peace. n the name of the father son and holy spirit.* Amen."

Don't be afraid to text a prayer to your kids or even ask them to text you with prayer requests. While it may take you longer to send your requests, your kids can probably hammer out a 5,000-word text in under 2 minutes!

Popcorn/Sentence Prayer

You've seen popcorn pop. As the kernels are slowly heated the excitement begins with a few random kernels popping and then, when it really gets going, you have multiple kernels popping at the same time. The popcorn prayer is designed to do the same thing. Make a list of "heated" sentences that need to be completed. Choose one and ask your family to quickly (like popcorn kernels popping) complete a sentence with a word or phrase. No introduction or amen is needed. Simply allow words to pop up randomly until every kernel has popped. Then go to the next sentence. Here are some examples.

Lord, I thank You for . . .
Lord, forgive me for . . .
Lord, help our family . . .
Lord please be with . . .
Lord, help me be more . . .
Lord, help me let go of . . .
Lord, give me the courage to . . .

Newspaper Prayer

When I was growing up, I remember that when we got the Sunday paper, Dad would take the front section, Mom would take the editorial pages, my oldest sister Sherri would take the comics, while my other sister Julie would take the entertainment section and I would take the sports. We would all go to different parts of the living room and kitchen and for the next 20 to 30 minutes you would hear different people say, as they were reading, things like:

- "Did you know . . ."
- "You'll never guess . . ."
- "I'll be . . ."
- "Yeah, right . . ."

And we would all stop and listen to what someone else had just read.

Using that idea, give each member of the household a section of the newspaper and 10 to 15 minutes to go through it, identifying any items that could become matters of prayer. For young children who are pre-readers or early readers, go through the paper with them, reading some of the headlines, looking at pictures and letting them select one or two to pray for.

Then gather together as a family and give each person a chance to share things they have identified that need prayer. One of the dangers with prayer is only praying for the things that directly affect you and forgetting to pray for the many things that need prayer in the world. The newspaper prayer will help your family engage in praying for things outside your immediate attention.

Laying on of Hands

Some of my most memorable times of prayer in my years in pastoral ministry are when people would lay hands on someone and pray. Laying on of hands in prayer is something we see throughout Scripture. Jacob blessed the sons of Joseph by laying his hands upon their heads (see Genesis 48:8-20), and Jesus similarly laid His hands on the sick (see Mark 5:23; 6:5; 7:32; 8:23,25; Matthew 9:18; Luke 4:40; 5:13; 13:13), as did the apostles (see Acts 9:12,17; 28:8; Mark 16:18). Yet, unfortunately for most, we see laying-on-of-hands prayer as something that is reserved for pastors, priests or lay professionals. But it's not. Try praying with laying on of hands in your family. You will find great benefits in it.

I'll never forget the phone call, "Mark, your dad has had a heart attack and is in the hospital." My wife and I were living in Iowa at the time and my parents lived three hours north of Minneapolis, Minnesota. Within 15 minutes of receiving that call my wife and I were in the car and on the way to the Brainerd, Minnesota, hospital. We gathered around my dad and laid our hands on him, praying for God to protect him from any further heart attacks and asking for healing. We didn't wait for any pastor to arrive, we simply prayed right there, in the same way the apostles did. Thankfully, those prayers were answered as we desired, and my dad made a strong recovery.

Laying on of hands is a form of prayer that is incredibly intimate and called for in times of distress or immediate need. By simply laying your hand on the head, shoulder or hand of the individual in need you are doing exactly what Christ would do. You are being His hands. Recently, I announced to the congregation of Ventura Missionary Church that I would be resigning as senior pastor, after six-and-a-half wonderful years, to become a full-time missionary called to serve the Faith at Home movement. Following the announcement, at all three services the members of the congregation came forward and laid hands on me and prayed over me. The comfort and encouragement I received through this time of prayer brought me peace and assurance that the Lord was with me.

If your husband comes home and announces that he has lost his job, gather around him as a family, lay your hands on him and pray that God will bring him comfort and peace until He provides a new job. If your wife tells you that she has been diagnosed with breast cancer, gather around her as a family and lay hands on her, asking the Lord to protect her and remove the cancer completely from her body through the treatment she will be undergoing, or by divine intervention. If your son is cut from the soccer team, or your daughter is betrayed by a friend at school, take a moment to lay your hands upon them and pray for them. You may think you are blessing them, and you are, but you will also find that you receive blessing.

Mealtime Prayer

Families are scattered in different directions throughout the day. If possible, schedule times when everyone can come together for at least one meal during the day. Use this opportunity of being together to pray together. My parents would always pray before every meal no matter where we were eating. That established a spiritually enriching ritual that remained with me into adulthood. At Bible camp, we had a myriad of mealtime prayers. Your family prayers may be spontaneous or memorized. Change the mealtime prayers as your children grow older. Here are a few you might want to choose from when you have younger children.

- Johnny Appleseed: *Oh the Lord is good to me, and so I thank the Lord, for giving me the things I need, the sun and the rain and the apple seed. The Lord is good to me. Amen.*

- God Is Great: *God is great, God is good, and we thank Him for our food. We're gonna thank Him in the morning, noon and night. We're gonna thank our God cause He's out of sight. We're gonna thank our God cause He's dynamite. Amen.*

- God Beloved (can be sung to the tune of "Are You Sleeping?"): *God beloved, God beloved, once again, once again. Thank You for our blessings, thank You for our blessings. A-A-men. A-A-men.*

- Superman (sung to the tune of "Superman"): *Thank you, Lord, for giving us food! Thank You Lord, for giving us food! For the friends that we meeee-eeeet, and the food that we eeee-eeeeat; thank You Lord, for giving us food.*

- Doxology: *Be present at our table, Lord. Be here and everywhere adored. These mercies bless and grant that we may strengthened for Thy service be. Amen.*

- For Life and Health: *For life and health and every good we give You thanks, O Lord.*

- Come, Lord Jesus: *Come, Lord Jesus, be our guest and let these gifts to us be blessed. Amen.*

You don't have to keep family prayer time to only before meals. Encourage conversation during your mealtimes. Let all family members take turns sharing something from their day. Talk with older children about events from the news. Before everyone leaves the table, pray together about various things that were shared around the table.

Email Prayer

When I travel overseas, many times my only way to communicate with my wife and daughter is through email. While I'm not able to pray with my daughter and wife directly, I can still receive their prayer requests, they can receive mine and we can pray for each other even though we are miles apart. When your child goes to college or is away for a period of time, use email as a way to share prayer requests and even write out your prayers for one another. I keep my daughter's email prayers because they are a source of encouragement to me when I'm away on a trip. Many young children have email accounts. Use these to stay connected to each other and to God through prayers. Set up your family as a group so you can send out an email to all of them with one message. You might want to print out the email exchanges and put them in a folder to pray about them when you are home together.

Monthly Prayer Calendar

As a family, write down 31 things to pray about each month and number each item. You might include certain people groups, like firefighters, schoolteachers, police officers, people in the military, the president of our country, your church, missionaries, neighbors, extended family members; specific things that need regular prayer, like the war on terrorism, homelessness or a cure for AIDS or cancer. Make a copy for each person in the family and keep a copy in a prominent place (refrigerator, kitchen table, hanging from the TV). Each day of the month, pray for the item that corresponds with that number. For young children who don't read, let them draw 31 pictures as their cue to pray each day.

Prayer Board

Use a whiteboard and let family members write prayer needs on it throughout the day. On a bulletin board, you could attach photos of friends, family members, teachers or missionaries. As you come together with your family at the end of the day, gather around the board and pray for each need or each person pictured on the board.

Spontaneous Prayer

Prayer can be continual conversation with God, which means you can pray anytime, anywhere. Instead of saying, "I'll pray for you," consider, "Let's pray for that right now." When a special concern or need arises, take time right then to say a prayer or call for silent prayer. Don't wait for the appointed prayer time.

Another way to engage in spontaneous prayer is through teachable moments where you come across a situation that shakes or shapes you as a family, and instead of simply letting it pass, you take a moment to discuss it and then pray about it. For example, at Christmas time we see a lot homeless people around the local store we frequently shop at. One time, as we were leaving, we were waiting at a stop sign with a homeless man standing right next to us for that period of time. The silence in the car was deafening and you could tell that we were all wrestling with whether or not we should roll down the window and give him some money.

Instead of not saying anything, I simply asked, "Hey, Malyn, are you wondering why we, as Christians, aren't giving money to this homeless person?" Her response was an instantaneous "Yes." My wife works for a homeless agency, and she was able to explain how panhandling actually perpetuates homelessness by keeping people from going to the places that truly want to help them get out of their homeless situation. Afterwards, we said a prayer for the person we saw standing there and for all the homeless people, as well as for the homeless agencies in our community. Spontaneous, teachable moments are great opportunities for prayer for the whole family.

Christmas or Birthday Card Prayers

Once, when I was leading a parenting workshop in Canada, and I asked the participants to share ways they had experienced prayer in their household, one woman raised her hand and shared that her family takes Christmas cards they receive each year and puts them in a box. Then, each week after church, they pull out a card and pray for the family or individual who sent the card. What a great idea! You may also want to send a card that every family member signs to that individual/or family, telling them that your family prayed for them.

The Prayer Hand

One way some people have used to remember different ways to pray is to trace your hand or write on the fingertips of an old glove, one per finger: praise God; thank God; confess your sins; ask God, pray for others. Spend a few moments on each different type of prayer during one prayer session. As your child grows older and has his or her own prayer times with God, this will be a good visual to keep the conversation in balance and not spend the whole time only asking God for things.

Prayer Songs

Music is an expression that works well with prayer because it touches emotions and helps when words aren't enough. Many prayers in the Bible have been put to music. Your family might know some from songs your church sings during worship services. If your children are very young, talk to their Sunday School teachers and find out what prayer songs they are singing at church so you can sing them at home. Ask your older children who their favorite Christian artists are and find songs they sing that are expressions to God. Some songs can be downloaded or listened to on the Internet. Some could be purchased. You could put your own prayers to familiar tunes. Use music in your prayer times with your family to express your heart. Your family might enjoy singing or just listening and praying along with prayer songs.

Prayer Art

Children often enjoy creating things and using a variety of senses in expressing themselves. Look for ways your family can pray while engaging in other activities. Young children might enjoy making things from God's creation with Play-Doh and talking to God about it. For example, after making a flower, they might pray, "Wow, God! You made so many pretty flowers." Older children might paint a scene from God's creation and express worship to their Creator.

Bedtime Prayer

The end of the day can be a special time for families. As activities and evening routines get completed, children of all ages are often ready to talk about their day and things that concern them. Sometimes this happens around the table during evening snacks or once everyone is ready to settle in bed. Allow enough time before lights out to engage in meaningful conversation and prayer. A great way to begin is to start by asking the question, "What were your highs and lows today? What was something that was great and something not so good?" What are you looking forward to about tomorrow? What are you worried about?" Spend time together taking these things to God in prayer. The next night, talk about how things went and how you saw God's work in different situations you prayed about.

Characteristics of God

Start with the words, "God is . . ." and make a list of God's characteristics. God is powerful, great, creative, and so on. Then take some time to discuss the ways you see those characteristics in God and in each other. Talk as a family about stories and verses from the Bible where God shows how you know God has that characteristic. Praise God for who He is and pray for one another that each family member could grow to be more Christ-like. For example, you might talk about how "God is love," read 1 Corinthians 13, talk about Jesus dying on the cross, and pray for family members to have more of His love in their hearts and express that love toward people they come in contact with.

Prayer Walks

Take family walks around your neighborhood or school or local track. As you walk, pray for the neighbors or the teachers and students at the school or any other topic you choose as a family to pray about. You could even take a prayer journal with you and whenever you cross paths with someone you could simply tell them that you are on a prayer walk and ask if they have any prayer requests/needs you could pray for. You will be amazed how many people will appreciate the fact that you are willing to pray for them. It's also a great way to get to know your neighbors!

Prayer Maps

If you have a world map or globe, spend some time as a family praying for different countries and people groups. Older children might want to do a little research on the Internet to find out information, including current news, faith systems, economic situations about the area so you could target your prayers to that area's needs. If you know missionaries or your church supports missionaries, find on the map where they live and pray for them.

Postures of Prayer

Try different body positions when you pray. The Bible describes people standing, sitting, kneeling and lying on the floor. You can pray with your head bowed and eyes closed or your eyes open and your head and hands raised to the sky. Some children may have difficulty sitting still for a period of time. Moving around while you pray might work better for them.

Peer Prayers

As your children grow, friends and peers become more influential in their lives. These relationships will affect your child's desires for spiritual things. Use your family prayer times to pray for your children's peers. Take a class photo or school yearbook and spend time praying together for groups or individuals in the pictures. Use the prayer time as opportunities to pray for the children or their families who are struggling in some way. Teaching your children to intercede for others will build lifelong habits of praying for others. Pray for and with your children that they will make good choices in the friends they get close to. When they talk about problems of a child at school or someone they don't like, listen to them, and then suggest that you pray together for that child.

As you can see, there are many ways to pray. For more ideas, visit faithbeginsathome.com and click on the Take It Home tab. Then go to the "At Home Prayer" tab and you will find many other prayer ideas. Pick the style of prayer that works for you. Keep adapting, keep changing and keep talking to your friends about the different ways they are praying. Most importantly, keep praying! If you have a good mealtime, bedtime or anytime prayer idea, please add it to the page so we can keep learning from one another.

Prayer List

Date	Requested by	Prayer Request (be specific)	Date Answered

Final Words

Chapter 1 gave you an overview of the biblical importance of prayer. You know that prayer can help you "enjoy long life" as a family. Chapter 2 gave you a peek into a couple of homes and you saw what a difference prayer makes in families that choose to pray together. Chapter 3 gave you principles for making prayer in your family successful. Chapter 4 gave you lots of ideas for praying together. All that is left for you to do is pray.

My final word of encouragement to you is to avoid making prayer a big, heavy, daunting thing to do as a family. Enjoy prayer. Incorporate it into your everyday life. Be creative with prayer and realize that all prayer is honoring to God as long as you are talking to Him.

Be warned that Satan is going to do two things to prevent you from praying. First he's going to make it difficult for you in the beginning. The hardest time you do something is the first time. Yet, each time you do it, you get better at it and it gets easier and more natural. It's the same with prayer. Don't fall for Satan's lies that you're not a good pray-er when the first couple of times don't go as well as you want them to go. Prepare yourself right now that the first few days and weeks may not be easy or natural. It will get easier—trust me. They say it takes 21 days to establish a new habit, so give yourself 21 days or 21 tries before you evaluate how it is going. Second, Satan is going to try to take away your passion and time for prayer.

Be encouraged, because greater in you is Jesus than anything Satan could use to try to distract you (see 1 John 4:4). Jesus desires to have conversation with you. He wants you to know Him better. He wants to help you and your family. Jesus used a word with his disciples 11 times in 7 verses of John 15. Remember, He was talking with His most devoted followers. They had been with him for over three years, yet He still had one important point He wanted to get across to them before He went to the cross. Do you know what that message was? REMAIN. Eleven times in seven verses He said, "Remain in me." Why did Jesus need to admonish His most fully devoted followers to remain in Him? Because He knew they would be tempted to fall away.

Jesus has the same message for you—*remain*. You will be tempted to fall away from your faith and the things that keep you closely connected to God. That is definitely the case with prayer. So hang in there—remain. If you find yourself getting complacent with one form or style of prayer, make a change. Keep your prayer life and relationship with Christ fresh and you will be blessed.

Finally, your prayer life will impact the prayer life of your children and your children's children. If you want your children to have a strong prayer life, make sure you have a strong prayer life. Deuteronomy

6:5-7 says, "Love the LORD your God with all your heart and with all your soul and with all your strength. These commandments that I give you today are to be upon your hearts. Impress them on your children." Did you notice where these "commandments" have to exist in you before they can be impressed on your children? They have to exist in YOUR HEART. You cannot pass something on to your children that you don't have yourself. The best thing you can do for your children is to set an example for them through the way you joyfully and continually engage in prayer. They will be impressed with that and it will leave an impression that will last their entire lifetime. Proverbs 22:6 says, "Train a child in the way he should go, and when he is old he will not turn from it."

May the Lord bless you and keep you as you begin your life of prayer as an individual and as a household. May the Lord make His face shine on you and be gracious to you as you pray. And may the Lord look upon you with favor and give you peace in and through prayer. In the name of the Father, and of the Son and of the Holy Spirit. Amen.

Acknowledgments

I want to thank all of the people at Gospel Light/ Regal Books who have faithfully supported the Faith@Home movement, even before it was a movement. They create resources like this that will help people bring prayer back into their everyday lives at home. I especially want to thank my editor, Jean Lawson, who not only edited this resource but also provided some of the great prayer ideas. And finally, I want to be sure to give credit to our Lord and Savior Jesus Christ who is the one who deserves all the credit for anything that is gained through this resource. God is my inspiration. I am simply an instrument through which He has chosen to work.

MARK A. HOLMEN

To find out more about Mark Holmen's speaking
engagements and to learn more about the
Faith@Home movement, visit faithathome.com.
Mark is available to speak to parents and church
leaders about how to be a faith-at-home focused
individual, family and church. For more information,
please contact Mark at mark@faithathome.com.

Also Available from
Mark Holmen

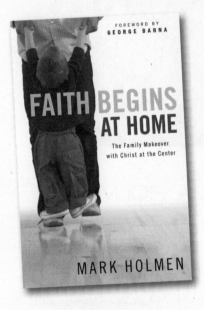

In *Faith Begins at Home*, Mark Holmen shows how becoming the strong, joy-filled and healthy family that God intended begins with parents establishing their homes as the primary place where faith is nurtured. In this engaging book, you will learn about the importance of your and your spouse's walk with the Lord; of using the gifts and experiences of grandparents, elders and mentors in the family; and of the role the church should play with families. Filled with a wealth of practical ideas, inspirational stories and biblical truth, *Faith Begins at Home* will inspire, motivate and equip you to help your family succeed.

Faith Begins at Home
ISBN 978.08307.38137
ISBN 08307.38134